Shape Shift

poems by

Shelley Minden

Finishing Line Press
Georgetown, Kentucky

Shape Shift

ACKNOWLEDGMENTS

This book would never have shape-shifted into reality without the teachers,
staff, and students of Seattle's Hugo House, especially Deborah Woodard,
Anastacia Tolbert, Rebecca Brown, JT Stewart, Joan Leegant, Richard
Chiem, and Eva Maria Sher. I also thank my late teacher and friend, Pesha
Joyce Gertler.

Publisher: Leah Maines
Editor: Christen Kincaid
Cover Art: Elsa Mora, www.elsamora.net
Author Photo: Ann Emanuel
Cover Design: Elizabeth Maines McCleavy

Printed in the USA on acid-free paper.
Order online: www.finishinglinepress.com
also available on amazon.com

Author inquiries and mail orders:
Finishing Line Press
P. O. Box 1626
Georgetown, Kentucky 40324
U. S. A.

Table of Contents

Her Words

She sits down to write. Brick walls loom. The moon climbs a black hill. Her mind is plain sky: no wit, no words. She writes: *"I am here! I am here!"* Turns her head up down, side to side. Will the roof fall, floor rise, walls press in? She leans back in her chair, then rears up, steps through the door and walks, then runs in the unfurling night.

Tell It Forwards

The pen might be a gun for how her hand shakes. Thoughts whirl from her grasp. Beyond the grimed window, bricks rise from concrete. The moon trudges along its black arc of night. She grips the pen, writes the second-most forbidden words: *"I am here!"* Writes them again, black ink on white paper. Her head is a bobble-doll's, checking walls, ceiling, floor. Will her world collapse?

Too wired to sit, she bursts through the door. Outside, the moon is unveiled. Hardworking, it must climb far, puffing under a backpack of clouds before the long slide down. She runs; streets unfold beneath her feet like a fan that opens forever. Is she afraid? Excited? Proud of herself, as if she's switched on a light and shone like the moon?

Tell It Backwards

She runs. Not afraid, although it is a city and dark, except for lights in the tall buildings and the giant streetlight of the moon. There are no limits to this night, this sky, the scope of her adventure. She runs and the streets are empty, she is alone like one black word on a wide white page. The moon, a writer now, watches. Is it pondering words, will it send them, glowing, through the night's dark pages?

Tell It Slant

This galaxy has seen it all. But it might glance at this woman running, afraid and brave, that far-away moon, that night that is smaller than a star speck, yet seems infinite to the woman, even to the moon, which climbs as if its life depends on it, as if the darkness below were quicksand, not knowing it shines a way for the woman looking up at it, not knowing it shines.

I. Tell It Forwards

Shape-Shifting

Get a flower bulb and a shovel and dig a hole in the ground. Aim toward China, unless you're already in China, in which case, tunnel toward Mexico.

Keep going. Pile up enough dirt to fill your closet minus the space occupied by the books lying open on your bedroom floor. In other words, shovel a volume of earth corresponding to the product of your latitude and longitude divided by the sum of all the numbers in your date of birth.

Sit in the deepest part of the hole and tell the bulb your most tender story. Then let the bulb tell a story to you. If you can't hear its story, think what your story might be if you were an unbloomed tulip. Write a prayer for the bulb. (If you forgot to bring a pencil and paper with you, climb back up and get them because this is important.) Write why you think you are on this earth and who you think you are. Write the last dream you had before starting digging, then write the ten thousand things that fill your mind. Put your writings on the ground and pile the dirt over them. When you are almost at the top, plant the bulb.

Now go home. Tell your boss you're sick and spend a day at the ocean. Float on the water and watch the sky. Make up six new names for each shade of blue you can identify, including four describing iridescent colors on butterfly wings. At night, scan the stars. Figure out which things you had thought were stars are really planets. Pick one planet and watch it until you can tell which way it's moving.

Get back to your regular life. Grab an armful of mail and toss it in the Dumpster. Suck up to your boss to make up for all the time you missed while communing with garden supplies. Regale your coworkers with a fantastical tale involving a trek across a desert and a flash mob of bighorn sheep.

If after a while you feel something lurching inside you, like maybe you swallowed some tadpoles that have turned into leaping frogs, just eat some flies to keep them occupied. If a skin or wall or other constraining thing emerges all around you, hire a stunt double to make appearances for you while you lie on some grass or dangle by your knees from a tree limb. If you awaken one morning with two crinkly appendages that are as long as your entire body and seem to have replaced your arms, just stretch them out and flap them to get the circulation going. Then, just fly.

In Paris

Paris is a painting. One sun glows and she glows. In Paris they glow.

In Paris trees drink sky. Swallow blue sky swallow black sky swallow sky with swallows. Trees swallow sun and sky in gardens. Along the boulevard trees swallow sky. Trunks of trees promenade. Trunks promenade on the west of the boulevard on the east of the boulevard, swallowing sky. Inside the sky fly branches of trees, branches and leaves, leaves and blossoms, blossoms and birds; east and west and in moonlight. In the sky branches touch branches touch leaves touch blossoms touch wings.

In Paris is Gertrude. In Paris is Alice.

Je suis ici! Ah Alice! Ah Gertrude! Ici? Je suis ici aussi! Ah le ciel! Ah les étoiles!
Bonne amie mon amie mon amour! C'est beau, c'est belle, c'est toi, c'est moi!
Bonjour le jour! Salut la nuit! Je t'aime mon amante! C'est belle, c'est ça!
Ah le soleil! Ah les oiseaux ! Bonjour Gertrude, bonne nuit Alice, c'est ça!
Nous nous aimons toujours, c'est bon, c'est bonne, c'est belle, c'est ça!
Gertrude bonne amie mon amie, Alice bonne amie mon amie!
La lune brille sur nous, elle est belle, c'est ça!
La pluie tombe sur nous, c'est ça!
Gertrude c'est bon, Alice c'est belle!
C'est toi! C'est moi!

Gertrude	Alice
in Gertrude	Alice B. Toklas
Gertrude Ste	Alice Baby
Mlle. Stein	las Wifey Mlle.
Mlle. Gertrude	Toklas Tok
ey Gertrude	ous Alice B.
n Gertrude Lov	las Baby Preci
Gertrude Stei	Mlle. Alice Tok
Gertrude Stein	Alice B. Toklas

3

Oak Leaves

Feathers of the forest
Now—lace on paving stones
Their rat tails bridge crevices
One curls as a cocoon—
Who burrows there, sprouting wings?

        The ice queen casts her spell
As thorough as snow
But an oak leaf dares trespass.

Rescued

from the California yard
barbed wire imprisoning
a strip of thin grass
two round bowls: one grain, one water
eyeing the sky.

Of humankind, some tell,
wise thoughts alone
might make
a heaven of hell.

But a hippo
even a pygmy hippo
needs what it needs:
needs water
trickling down rocks
needs brush
throbbing with bird wings
needs mud holes:
sacred as prayer.

Today she lumbers
from the wide pool of water
to the pond of mud
sinks until just two nostrils meet the sky.

Heaven is surely mud
on webbed toes brief tail ponderous jaw
lifting
    lapping
like the licking
of one hundred mothers' tongues.

Visitation

Shelley looked up to discover a seal in the room. The seal seemed completely at home, like the room was its beach with big rocks and other seals and rows of waves breaking their own frothy backs, just to regroup and do it again. But it was Shelley's room—her small studio apartment in Somerville, Massachusetts. She wondered if this was her book or her dream or maybe somehow the TV had gotten so big it had become the room instead of just being in it. She got up from her mattress on the floor and moved close to it. It was a very smooth seal, just as she had thought a seal would be. It smelled a little like fish, and there were wet spots on the floor beside it.

The seal turned its head toward Shelley and they studied each other's faces. Shelley felt a need to explain her circumstances. See, this is how I live, she said, but it might just be for now. Picture this place filled with people, all kinds of people, except of course no mean people, and they are all my friends! It would be a little crowded, but we would be so friendly we wouldn't mind. And lovers, did I mention lovers? Picture a heartbroken outgoing lover, a promising potential lover, and a real true-blue right-in-this-minute lover. And there would be my work. I don't mean work that pays the rent but my big creative writing that would pour out of me like I had a magic pen with a genie in it.

When Shelley at last paused for breath the seal made a loud sound, in fact the loudest sound Shelley suspected had ever occurred in her tenure in this apartment. Her upstairs neighbor, Louisa, banged on the ceiling with her broom. OK, Shelley conceded, it might sound a little unrealistic. Oh, wait, are you hungry? When did you last eat?

Shelley dug through cupboards while the seal roamed the apartment, touching its nose and whiskers to the mattress and then the desk with its typewriter and unpaid bills. Shelley found four cans of tuna, two of salmon, and a tin of sardines, while the seal uncovered three empty candy wrappers and a collection of alphabet mysteries.

Shelley dumped the food on the floor.

To feed a wild seal in your own apartment is to dive from a green-tinged ice floe into the open ocean, going deeper and deeper as the water gets darker and darker, until suddenly you're swimming among blinking stars like a fast-moving planet in the night sky.

To clean up after a 300-plus-pound seal has consumed many cans of food in your apartment is to suffer paroxysms of doubt in your own capabilities interspersed with terror at the thought of what your landlord might eventually discover until finally you're doing it, with all the towels you own and the bucket you naively purchased for washing some lacy thing you've never even worn and you've actually got a rhythm, with one side contracting in self-doubt and the other expanding into action, leading you to a turning point at which you've knitted together your whole life's contradictions.

It was very dark outside when Shelley finished cleaning. She pushed her mattress next to the seal. Shelley knew a seal visitation was unlikely to last forever, maybe not even for one night. But the seal was here now, having churned its way through the planet to manifest at her side. Shelley closed her eyes and leaned her head against a flipper. She and the seal dreamed, the seal of the blissful chill of ice and of its own pups making their first little dives into the sea. Shelley dreamed that her coworkers put her into a zoo for human specimens lacking in private education, then she dreamed of the Rocky Mountains bulging like angry muscles against the surrounding plains where her parents lived, the undulating ships of Boston Harbor, and Paul Revere on his horse calling out whichever way it was that they were coming. But it was in the quiet spaces between dreams when it happened— when some unnamable entity shifted, dispersed, and coalesced inside her like a murmuration of starlings, leaving the print of a wild seal on her consciousness, something she would be able to perceive for many years to come.

II. Tell It Backwards

Sloth and Torpor Tour the Universe

Sloth and Torpor slumber cocoon-like in a spaceship of carbon and titanium, its cone pointing away from Earth, engulfed by the universe, which buffets, ices, and generally toys with them as it would anything that has ventured far from the protective gravity of a solid planet.

SLOTH
(Rousing to lift his head for his first glimpse of Space)
I thought I failed the physical.

TORPOR
Was there a test?

SLOTH
They asked me to open my eyes. I could pry the right one open, but when I tried for the left they both sank like anchors.

TORPOR
They didn't ask me anything. They dragged me by my hair.

SLOTH
Oh the dreaded hair drag. I've been there brother.

TORPOR
I said to them, gentlemen, feel free to take my hair, I never liked it anyway, but please leave the rest of me to continue my nap. Then I thought I did keep napping, only now I'm here.

SLOTH
Why do you think they picked us?

TORPOR
(After an hour's rest) Maybe we're authorities on something.

SLOTH

Is there anything you're an expert on?

TORPOR

Well, getting fired, getting evicted, sleeping on the street and having kids kick me. Are you good at anything?

SLOTH

I can sleep anywhere. Maybe that's why they picked us. I slept through a prison sentence once.

TORPOR

(Admiringly) Really, what did you do?

SLOTH

I don't think I did anything, but it didn't seem worth arguing about. They were so desperate to find someone who would go, so I made them happy and it wasn't that bad there.

Years pass.

SLOTH

What do you miss the most?

TORPOR

Sleeping.

SLOTH

We've been sleeping here.

TORPOR

I miss sleeping where I stay in one place and breathe real air and know if it's day or night. I miss hearing people getting up and going to work and knowing I'm not going with them.

SLOTH

Oh yes, that's a good one. And waking to a ringing phone, burying myself under the covers and going back to sleep. (Sighs a deep sigh.)

TORPOR

There's something there.

SLOTH

Is it worth opening my eyes for?

TORPOR

Well, it's a little speck, like a grain of salt, only red.

SLOTH

I think I need to rest some more before I look at it.

TORPOR

Just picture it then, imagine something like a round grain of rice. No, something like a pea.

SLOTH

You're making me hungry. What happened to those meals that popped out from the walls? Aren't we due for one?

TORPOR

I'm hungry too. Well, focus on this, a red-brown thing, maybe as big as a plum. Actually a grapefruit. (Pause.) Man oh man.

SLOTH

What is it?

TORPOR

It's as big as a dinner plate.

Enter a silence like a second spaceship, one that burrows under the skin of the universe and tears through its tissue, so that for the briefest possible fraction of space-time the majestic universe itself flinches.

SLOTH

We're crashing into it aren't we?

The Wall

My sister and I are building a wall of sand. We take the sand from the beach, where it is wet from the tide, and carry it carefully home. We have a model: The Great Wall of China, and a name: The Great Protector.

Each day we bring fresh sand in teaspoons stolen from our parents' kitchen. The wall grows and grows. It rains down sand yet rises in height. Parts of it are as thin as a seashell.

Each spoonful of sand is an offering, a prayer. O Great Wall, please hold us safe, please guard and protect us.

We've been building the wall for so long we can't remember not having been building the wall when we see it: the wall has been breached! Our uncle has breached the wall. O wall, please save us!

We gather more sand and it seems to attach solidly
when it is wet. But then it dries and pours down in rivulets. It collapses in rain, it dissipates in wind.

Oh wall, oh wall, oh wall.

The Child

Not wanted, the child popped out anyway.
Averting her eyes, she saw everything just the same.
The white cat, with its soft tail and aggrieved meow.
The snail in its intricate shell, each eye on its own conveyance!
The big green car, packed with despair.
Big sisters, one two and three, they hate me.
This place is called L.A.; we call it far away.

When I was a child I saw and didn't see, knew but didn't know
Everything I saw and didn't see and knew and didn't know
warred inside me as I grew.

The Mystery

There was no mother, not even the ticking clock
they wrapped in towels to deceive the dog.
There was the glare
　　of light or dark or hate
　　I can't remember which.
I've heard: look only forward. Still,
with so many shards and each so small
what was broken is a mystery.

War Is Over
After Allen Ginsberg

Mom,
that school in rural Illinois—
where every kid got valentines but you
    the Jew—
it's gone now Mom.
It's a shopping mall now.
They sell Frappuccinos there now.

That teacher, who hated your dad, hated Jews,
hated you, she's buried now.
Her eyes don't burn like cigarettes in skin now.
They don't see grass or clouds, they're gone now.
She's only bones now, lying on sticks of wood
or maybe plain dark earth we could hold in our hands.

Mom, your father is dead now.
His fine script is no more.
His bald head doesn't preen in mirrors now.
His fist, those four uncrossable mountain peaks,
gone now.

    And Mom, your mother—
who spooned you cream from milk
who let you bring the kitten in the tub
who blamed her black eye on the door
her burned arm on the iron—
she's in Eternity, Mom.
She's with Eleanor Roosevelt and Emma Goldman now
Oh the times they must have!

Please Mom, put down the vacuum cleaner, the telephone,
the dish rag, the car keys.
I've poured us cups of tea.
See how they glisten, just like Issa said.
Please, with your spirit eyes
see the steam float up and climb the sky
like the spider you once sang to me about
and meet a cloud as softly
as heaven might in time meet you and me.
See how the cloud's tears cross
the sky's long weathered face, falling
finally, at your door.

Sproul Hall, 1965

I was young but I was there
visiting an older sister.
We saw the students blowing bubbles near the gate
watched the bubbles,
buoyed by the exuberance of the day
    the radiance of the future
        the lift of pot smoke thick as mist,
soar above Sproul Hall.

No country here for the Mean Girls of home
couture clothes, reserved positions
on the cheerleading squad.

Dazzled, I followed my sister
beneath the spreading bubbles
beyond Telegraph
with its colored beads and flowers
 to her rented cubbyhole.
She'd plastered the walls with peace signs
lectured me on napalm
but we didn't share our own wars.
Her, young, alone, afraid.
Me, layered in fear and doubt
encumbered as an Arctic traveler.

Now, after all these decades
my sister claims her home with the religious
and I've spent long years wandering
extricating fear
excavating ardor
and finally feel the sun.

Still, I'd crawl back under all those airless
layers, to be able to believe again
that a great wave of peace has crested
and bombs will turn to butterflies
and everyone, together, with none neglected
will rise up into love
like bubbles wreathed in pot smoke
above Sproul Hall.

III. Tell It Slant

Half-Moon Yodel

After Frank Stanford

Cabs crawl down Main Street
like a thin line of ants.
A Northern flicker, instinct taught my cry.
Intransigence fuels it.
You are a red rickshaw
pedaled by the rising moon.
I am a late-day sunray, flickering
like the last match in the box.

A storm is coming, they say
visiting like the priest does the dying.
I tell you this with my flicker cry
yodeling across the Sound.

Crime Seen

After the dioramas of Frances Glessner Lee: Nutshell Studies of Unexplained Death

There's a tick, then smashing tinkling falling, a bird's frightened flight, thin mirror of metal, then tock.

Wallpaper roses edged with ice. A man's breath, blood-red, like monks chanting ohmmm, ohmmm, keeping going until the world ends. There's a window—the moon morphs into meteors and is gone.

Look up! The ceiling fixture, rays of sun and shadow spinning; it's God's eye, watching.

The firmament tips and Earth, untethered, green and blue and mist, rolls off the edge like a marble. *So sorry!*

Now hovering in air she sees it all: God at his peephole, her body on the floor (*so very sorry!*), even the broom in motion, the folding of the blue dress on itself, the clock uninterrupted.

Lisbon

Today I'm lucid, as if I were about to die
And had no greater kinship with things
Than to say farewell…
—Fernando Pessoa, "The Tobacco Shop"

With words, my kinship is a flame-
blue swampflower, half in mud half in sky and numerous other
fractions in a dream of a cloud shaped like a whale
that passes over Lisbon, drifting slowly like a parade balloon
dripping cloud dust on the Rua Augusta, conjuring swampflowers
that knock you dead with their strong swamp smell
zap you into eternity with their blue that might be sapphire
or the interior of a cupboard in sky openable by the knob
we call Sun but eternally tied to me with thread that can yank
me at whim send me flying like a child's tooth to a doorknob
and maybe I will fly forever or maybe I'll be forever tethered
to the closed door of Lisbon biting swampflower air

Shelley Minden is a cross-genre writer and storyteller. She was born in Los Angeles and studied biology in school, earning a Bachelor of Science degree from the University of Colorado and a Master of Science degree from the University of Oregon. She worked for many years as a medical writer and editor. She now lives in Seattle, where she has turned her focus to the creative realm. Her poetry has appeared online, and she has read her work at several Seattle venues. She is an active member of the Hugo House, a center for writers. *Shape Shift* is her first book.

www.ingramcontent.com/pod-product-compliance
Lightning Source LLC
LaVergne TN
LVHW051614080426
835510LV00020B/3288